My Phonics Words

The Sound of AW

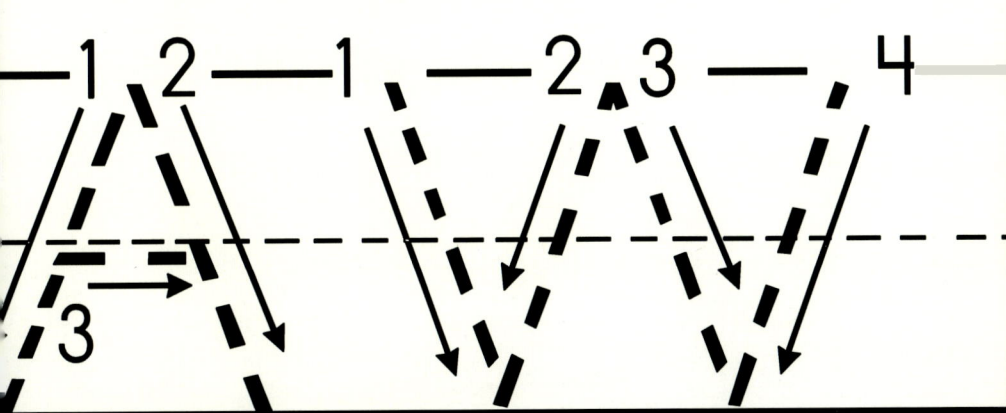

CHRISTINA EARLEY

A Little Honey Book

Crabtree Publishing
crabtreebooks.com

paw

saw

crawl

fawn

CAREGIVER TIPS AND ACTIVITIES

PHONICS INSTRUCTION

Phonics is the relationship between letters and their sounds. This is the basis for reading. It is the most important skill that beginning readers learn. Children who have phonics instruction become better readers and spellers.

All words are made up of sounds. The word "dog" has three sounds. Each letter is one sound. The word "light" has three sounds. The letters "igh" are one sound. The English language uses 44 sounds to make all words. However, there are 26 letters in the alphabet. The vowels are a, e, i, o, u, and y at the end or in the middle of a word. The consonants are b, c, d, f, g, h, j, k, l, m, n, p, q, r, s, t, v, w, x, z, and y at the beginning of a word. Some letters make more than one sound. Other letters combine to make new sounds. This is like a code. When a child knows the code, he or she can sound out many words. This is decoding.

Phonics is one tool for reading words. It is important for students to learn words that do not follow phonics rules. These words are called sight words because they need to be remembered when the child sees them. The most common sight word lists are Dolch Sight Words and Fry Sight Words. By practicing both decodable words and sight words, children will become fluent and successful readers.

PHONICS ACTIVITIES

1. **Have a Ball:** One person holds a ball and calls out a letter name or sound. Then, they throw the ball to another person who says a word with that letter or sound. Then, that person calls out a letter name or sound and throws the ball.

2. **Rainbow Hop:** Write different letter sounds on colored pieces of paper. Use one sound on each paper. Tape the papers onto the floor in a line. Roll a die. Hop that many times along the papers. For the last hop, say the sound of the letter(s) and a word with that sound.

3. **Write the Rainbow:** Use a red crayon, pencil, or marker to write a letter sound on a piece of paper, saying the names of the letter(s) as you write them. Then, underline and say the sound. Repeat with orange, yellow, green, blue, and purple.

4. **Swat It:** Write letter sounds you are practicing on sticky notes. Place on a wall. Call out a letter or sound. The child uses a flyswatter to swat the note with that sound. You can also write words with the letter sounds on sticky notes.

5. **Detective:** Use your super detective skills to find words with a target letter sound in the world around you throughout the day. Do you see words with that letter sound in the book you are reading? Is it on your favorite box of cereal? How about at the grocery store?

6. **Clap It:** Choose a favorite song. Clap out each syllable (word part) of the words as you sing the song.

7. **Rhyme Time:** Say two words. If they rhyme, stand up. If they don't, sit down.

HANDS-ON PROJECT: MAGIC DOOR FOLDABLE

1. Place paper horizontally in front of you.
2. Fold over the left side to the center of the paper. Crease well.
3. Fold over the right side to the center of the paper. Crease well.
4. With both sides still folded, fold the top edge to the bottom edge.
5. Open once (both left and right will still be folded). Cut along the valley fold lines to create doors.

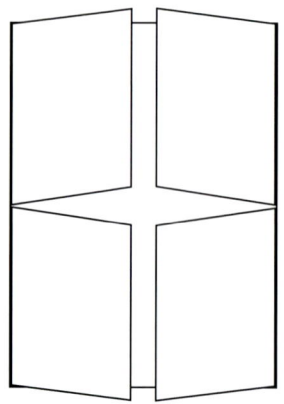

MAGIC DOOR FOLDABLE ACTIVITIES

1. Write a phonics word on the door. Draw a matching picture behind the door.
2. Draw a picture on the door. Write the matching phonics word behind the door.
3. Write the letter(s) of a sound on a door. Write matching words behind the door.
4. Draw a picture on the door. Behind the door, write letters that make a sound in the picture's name.
5. On the door, write a letter or letters that make more than one sound. Write words with the different sounds of the letter(s) behind the door.

HANDS-ON PROJECT: MINI BOOK

1. Place paper horizontally in front of you.
2. Fold right side edge over to left side edge. Make a crease. Keep closed.
3. Again fold right side over to left side. Make a crease.
4. Open once. Fold top edge to bottom edge. Crease.
5. Open paper completely. Fold left side over to right side. Use scissors to cut on the dotted line shown in Step 5 illustration.
6. Open paper completely. There should be a hole in the crease in the center of the paper.
7. Fold long edge top to long edge bottom.
8. Hold on short sides and push together. Crease.
9. Fold in half to finish book.

Step 5

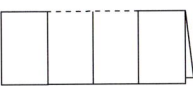
Step 7

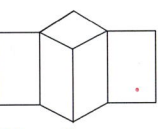
Step 8

Step 9

MINI BOOK ACTIVITIES

1. Write a phonics word on each page and illustrate each word.
2. Write a word on each page. Use a different color for the letter(s) of the sound you are working on.
3. Write a letter sound at the top of a two-page spread. Fill the spread with pictures whose names have the sound. Write the word under each picture.
4. Write a story using words with the letter sound you are working on.
5. Write a letter sound on a page. Write words that you find with that letter sound.

My Phonics Words
The Sound of AW

Written by: Christina Earley
Designed by: Niko Magaro
Series Development: James Earley
Editor: Kim Thompson
Proofreader: Candice Campbell
Educational Consultant: Marie Lemke M.Ed.

Photographs: Shutterstock: Eric Isselee: cover; BublikHaus: p.2; Thomas Hecker: p.3; Monkey Business Images: p.4; COULANGES: p.5; Danita Delimont: p.6; Lovy Pirate: p.7; Yellow Cat: p.8; Kovaleva_Ka: p.9; MarkoBr: p.10; Divelvanov: p.11

Crabtree Publishing

crabtreebooks.com 800-387-7650
Copyright © 2022 Crabtree Publishing
All rights reserved. No part of this publication may be reproduced, stored in a retrieval system or be transmitted in any form or by any means, electronic, mechanical, photocopying, recording, or otherwise, without the prior written permission of Crabtree Publishing.

Hardcover	978-1-0396-9510-8
Paperback	978-1-0396-4564-6
Ebook (pdf)	978-1-0396-5168-5
Epub	978-1-0396-5375-7
Read-along	978-1-0396-5582-9
Audio book	978-1-0396-5853-5

Published in Canada
Crabtree Publishing
616 Welland Ave.
St. Catharines, Ontario
L2M 5V6

Published in the United States
Crabtree Publishing
347 Fifth Ave
Suite 1402-145
New York, NY 10016

Library and Archives Canada Cataloguing in Publication
Available at the Library and Archives Canada

Library of Congress Cataloging-in-Publication Data
Available at the Library of Congress

Printed in the U.S.A./HF20220616/092022